THE SALES MANAGERS' FORUM

The Combination to the Vault for Sales Managers in the Car Business

JAMES A. ZIEGLER

ISBN Paperback: 979-8-89079-042-2
ISBN Ebook: 979-8-89079-064-4

Published by Peach State Press

FOREWORD

When the time came to select the retail automotive "subject matter expert", there was one name that was continually mentioned throughout my curriculum advisory board – "Why don't you ask, Jim Ziegler, the Alpha Dawg".

At Northwood University we are so pleased that Jim said yes. His leadership, expertise, inspiration, and classroom style are second to none. He knows what he teaches because he's done what he teaches in the real world, with real customers.

Jim is a friend, but more importantly he is a living resource that takes time to mentor students. And once again Jim has taken time to put his thoughts, stories, tips, and techniques into a book. Jim's expertise will be a must read for the future leaders in the Northwood University Automotive program. If you are the type of leader that wants practical knowledge, inspirational commentary, or just plain old fashioned, get it done, management tips: Read this book. Jim's style is straightforward, thought provoking, and like any good preacher/teacher, may make you a little uncomfortable at times. When that happens, you know you've picked up the right book.

Thank you, Jim, for all you do to advance automotive retail education.

Professor Elgie Bright
Chair - Automotive Marketing and Management
at Northwood University

WHO IS JM ZIEGLER, CSP, HSG, OG, THE ALPHA DAWG?

"Jim Ziegler helps people and organizations discover the power of developing and leveraging relationships for increased sales and profits"

> **James A. Ziegler, CSP, HSG** …Ziegler SuperSystems, inc. Lives in Chateau Elan Country Club Estates, Braselton, Georgia. For 49 years, Jim Ziegler's been a recognized industry, writer, magazine columnist, professional speaker, and super performer. Following a record-setting Sales Career as an F&I Manager/Director and General Sales Manager with some of the top automobile dealerships and groups in the country Jim Ziegler's credentials include…

- A record-setting manager with several of the top performing dealerships and groups in the country
- Associate professor teaching Automotive General Management at Northwood University
- Associate professor teaching Automotive F&I at Northwood university
- Worked with more than 15,000 dealerships nationwide.
- Eagle Scout
- Red Cross Certified Water Safety Instructor five years
- 125,000 Dealers, Managers and Executives attended his seminars since 1986.
- Teaches Seminars on F&I, Sales Management, Sales and Internet Marketing
- He's worked in more than 1000 showrooms in 200 cities in 49 states. (not Alaska yet)
- The featured opening keynote speaker 98 State Automobile Dealer Association Conventions

- rated in top 10 workshop speakers at 17 National NADA Conventions
- 2008 Keynote Speaker Australian National Auto Dealers Annual Convention in Brisbane Gold Coast, AU.
- featured speaker at 3 J.D. Power Roundtables
- opening keynote speaker 4 AICPA Conventions
- More than 150,000 friends and followers on Social Media (mostly automotive)
- Speaker at four Digital Dealer Conventions, including Opening Keynote Speaker at DD2
- Opening Speaker on the Big Stage Digital Dealer DD22 Tampa
- Featured Opening Speaker Digital Dealer 24 Orlando
- Widely Read National Columnist, Automotive Retail (www. AlphaDawgBlog.com)
- respected industry futurist and forecaster
- 14 Years as the original featured Columnist in Dealer Magazine
- Featured Columnist, five years, for Wards Dealer Business Magazine
- Lead Columnist for F&I/Showroom magazine (5 years)
- Featured Columnist for Auto Dealer Today magazine (5 years)
- writes for ADM Community and Dealer Elite online communities
- Prolific Automotive Blogger with hundreds of thousands of followers
- Jim's 25 **"Internet Battle Plan"** events were attended by thousands of dealers, managers, and automotive executives.
- 2006 **Toastmasters International Leadership National Award** for helping others in their career path
- Jim is regularly called on by top manufacturer executives for his input on dealer matters
- 2012 Jim was awarded the "Passion Award" for lifetime achievement in the industry

- 2012 Jim was awarded the 'AutoCon' lifetime achievement award
- Jim has been awarded the prestigious **Dealer's Choice Gold and Diamond Awards** as **Automotive Sales and Management Trainer of the Year Voted on by Dealers**.

  He is the only person to have won this highest-level award five times, 2014, 2015, 2016, 2017, and repeating in 2018

- **Recipient of the 2019 Edward Bobit Lifetime Achievement Award**
- Jim's online training platform, **ZieglerOnDemand.com** is FREE for dealers, managers, and Sales Professionals as well as BDC and internet managers featuring 1000's of video training modules by Jim as well as interviews with top industry personalities.

James A. Ziegler, CSP, The Alpha Dawg as a professional member of the National Speaker's Association as well as National Speaker's Association Georgia. In July 2001, Jim earned the prestigious *"Certified Speaking Professional"* (CSP) designation at the NSA National Convention in Dallas. Less than 1/3 of one percent of all professional speakers worldwide ever achieves this coveted honor, the association's highest earned award. In 2004, He earned the "Lifetime CSP Designation.

For more than 49 years, James A. Ziegler, CSP has researched, studied, and trained in the retail automobile business as surely as if he were studying for a Masters' degree in any other profession. He's the ultimate student of our industry; Ziegler exhibits intellectual dynamics and an incredible ability to perform at levels above the industry.

Jim Ziegler's future forecasting has claimed accuracy in the 95% + category for predicting industry trends and events before they happen. The best record in the industry.

Nobody has hands-on experience rivaling his accomplishments in the retail auto industry. Since March of 1986, Ziegler has done business with more than 15,000 dealerships nationwide and more than 125,000 Dealers, managers and factory executives have attended Jim's automobile dealer management seminars. Traveling more than 200 days a year, the man has physically worked in more than 1000 showrooms in no less than 200 cities in 49 states. (hasn't made it to Alaska yet)

As a retail consultant having worked with manufacturers and more than 1000 dealerships nationwide. He's been featured opening keynote speaker for 98 State Automobile Dealer Association Annual Conventions and has been consistently rated at the top of the top ten speakers at 17 National NADA Conventions

Jim was 2008 Keynote Speaker Australian National Auto Dealers Annual Convention in Brisbane Gold Coast.

James Ziegler is often interviewed, featured in articles by him or about him, and quoted as an industry expert by *Auto Dealer Monthly*, Reuters, *Automotive News, USA Today, Bloomberg News, Dow-Jones, Wards Dealer Business, F&I and Showroom magazine, Entrepreneur magazine and Success magazine, Newswire, Automotive Executive, RV Executive today, Auto Age, Auto Success, Dealer magazine, Atlanta Journal-Constitution, WSB television, BBC International Radio, Detroit News, and he's appeared on CNN.*

Ziegler's been the featured national magazine columnist for **F&I and Showroom Magazine** and also **Auto Dealer Today Magazine.** for more than 14 years Jim has been the spotlight featured monthly columnist **in DEALER Magazine** with his very popular, always controversial column **"The Dealer Advocate"**, previously the regularly featured columnist for **Wards Auto Dealer Business Magazine** and **Auto Age.**

Writing as a featured columnist for 5 different national magazines in the Car Business, Extremely popular with the Dealers and respected by the factories and industry insiders, the man has become an in-demand celebrity speaker in the retail automobile industry.

Ziegler is a cut above; the author of **The Prosperity Equation, New Millennium,** the secrets of what it takes to become wealthy, prosperous and a success in today's business world

Co-Workers described him as a "Hard Ass" manager. They might also say that James A. Ziegler is the best there is in the U.S. retail automobile business today. He's been described as that "In-Your-Face" sort of guy. Don't ask Ziegler a question if you're not prepared to hear the answer.

Maybe Jim doesn't take himself as seriously as all of that. Outrageous, with a deep sense of humor, Ziegler might be putting you on with the hats, jewelry, swagger, and over-the-top persona. Don't underestimate this guy; he's the real deal. His persona and brash mannerisms are carefully, deliberately crafted. Bob Danzig, president of Hearst Newspapers, once described Jim Ziegler as *"Strategic Audacity"*.

They'll tell you Jim Ziegler is honest, intellectual, and sincere, but; he is also one of the funniest human beings on the planet with his unique sarcasm brand of humor. His humor sneaks up on you and you'll find yourself laughing minutes later when that aha moment strikes you.

An early adopter, Jim's been using America Online since 1994, He smiles when people see his email address. You can contact Jim Ziegler at ZieglerSS@aol.com (706) 684-0010 or Jim's cell at (770) 851-2803, 9-5 Eastern US Time

Controversial, arrogant, egotistical, the man is a showman. Those who really know him will tell you Jim Ziegler is honest, intellectual, and sincere. They will also say that James A. Ziegler is the best there is in the retail automobile business today.

http://www.ZieglerOnDemand.com

http://www.ZieglerSuperSystems.com

Dear Dealer;

In a fiercely competitive marketplace the **losers** are quickly and permanently distinguished from the **winners.** A new retail automobile dealership has to be designed to maximize every sales opportunity, as that opportunity occurs. Therefore, one simple, yet vital question arises ...

"IS YOUR DEALERSHIP OPERATING AT IT'S POTENTIAL?"

In the Car Business since 1976, and in the consulting and training business since 1986, The Alpha Dawg issues you this guarantee...

"I Will Dramatically Increase Your Profits, Immediately!"

Jim's track record for hands-on, in dealership consultancy stands alone. There are hundreds of references from reputable dealers, and industry executives, and managers from dealerships of every type, large and small, across the country.

► Dramatic Increased Unit Sales
► Extreme Team Motivation
► F&I and Secondary Management
► Total Efficiency

► Amazing Increased Profitability
► Disciplined Management Style
► Operation Expense Control
► Total Profitability

"AN AUTOMOBILE DEALERSHIP WITHOUT A MEASURABLE AND ORGANIZED SELLING PROCESS IS LIKE A LOST PUPPY ON AN INTERSTATE HIGHWAY"

WHAT DOES IT TAKE TO GROW A DEALERSHIP TO IT'S ULTIMATE POTENTIAL?

Jim Ziegler has a reputation for growing dealerships to the *'Big Numbers'* in a very short amount of time. Ziegler's management strategy is simple, **"Evaluate and Execute"**.

From 100 units a month to 500 units, or 400 units to 1000 units, the secret formula is to access the dealership's capability and then *"Act Like You're Already Doing It."*

Once you have determined the dealership has the potential to sell 500 units a month, then hire the staff, stock up the inventory, and advertise with 500 units in mind. In other words, have enough sales and management persons to handle it, have enough inventory, and advertise as if you are already selling 500 units. Don't try to gradually achieve 500, but rather *"Act as if it's already happening"*.

- An advanced, modern 'Road to the Sale' selling procedure designed to control and measure the sale with increases in unit sales, sales gross, and F&I/Leasing profitability. The 'Road to the Sale" didn't die or become obsolete, we just added 'technology tools', Digital Retail, CRM, and 'websites' into the process.

- Procedures on how to handle banks, credit unions, and cash sale conversions to retain finance profit and control the deal more effectively

- Desk-controlled Sales Procedures, a minimum of one out of five deals at or above full list profitability. The dealership's mantra becomes "All of the Money, All of the Time!" We will never miss an opportunity to make a sale

- Customer interviews built into the process with customer-friendly word tracks to get more deals approved through scientific, professional deal investigation

- Customer tracking and follow-up procedures

- Improved hiring, firing, training, and promoting procedures

- Convert qualified customers to retail leasing

- Increased extended service contract sales and profitability

THE SALES MANAGER

Of all of the positions in the front-end operation of the modern retail automobile dealership, the sales manager's roll is the most crucial to the success or failure of the dealership.

Without the sale of an automobile nothing else would happen. There wouldn't be any cars to finance or repair. There wouldn't be any customers to follow up or any paperwork to process. Every job in the dealership, including the dealer, depends on the ability of the sales manager and the efforts of his/her department.

In recent years the automobile business has become more and more competitive as new dealerships seem to spring up on almost every street corner. **In Atlanta, Georgia alone over seventy new dealerships have been constructed in the five-year period between 1996-2001** and there are more than twenty more in the planning stages at this very minute.

Now, more than ever, the sales manager in a retail automobile dealership has to be a highly trained professional with the ability to control and supervise the entire sales effort. The person in this position must be intelligent and able to think quickly on their feet.

Although the unwritten prime directives in the car business are..." **Hold the gross and move the units** "...a sales manager in today's sales environment must have a variety of other functional talents in addition to salesmanship.

All too often some hotshot sales manager pictures him/herself as the quarterback who personally runs every play and takes all of the bows and all of the applause.

In truth, the better sales managers are the coaches who send In the plays to the Sales Professionals who are on the front lines. It takes **planning** and **organization** as well as **discipline** to build this unified team.

The days of the "hotshots" are fading. **In truth, we cannot tolerate anything but the highest ethic and integrity in our industry and most "hotshots" do not possess such characteristics in today's dealerships.**

Today's sales manager is a motivated, disciplined individual with proven talents and abilities...a professional who studies his/her profession as surely as if they were studying for a master's degree in any other profession.

SALES MANAGER IS A TITLE OF RESPECT AND DIGNITY.

The title of sales manager is earned through performance and example, not just because someone has printed that title on your business card.

It is also a title of authority and command...a good manager has the ability to make a quick decision and the backbone to see that it is carried out.

The primary duties of a sales manager can be broken down into four categories, which are

(1) Planning

(2) Evaluating

(3) Coordinating

(4) Organizing

All of the factors that have anything to do with the operation of the sales department...everything that the job requires...will fall within the boundaries and definitions of those categories. As this chapter develops, you will begin to realize why the sales manager has to be multi-talented to effectively handle all of the diverse duties that the position requires.

You may have noticed that I haven't singled out whether or not the sales manager is a new car sales manager or a used car sales manager, a general sales manager or even an F&I Manager. For the purposes of this textbook, a sales manager can be any manager who is responsible for the duties of a sales manager; usually, we will be referring to the job description and the duties of the new car sales manager. When a manager becomes involved with directing the sales force, that manager must have authority and respect.

A 'Sales Manager' is a title of Dignity, Authority, and Respect. If You don't have all three, you are Not a Sales Manager.

THE SALES MANAGER

Planning Evaluating Coordinating, and Organizing

A. Planning

1. Long-range and short-range goals for the sales department. (accurate forecasting)

2. Staffing requirements

   a) Hiring-firing-training-promoting

3. Inventory projections

   a) Special packages...unit balance
   b) Projected sales and days' supply
   c) Seasonal units and hot sellers
   d) Aged inventory

4. Profit projections

   a) Front gross
   b) Bonuses and compensation/commissions
   c) Advertising costs

5. Sales Projections

6. Working standards, ethics, procedures, policies of the sales department

   a) Setting down rules and guidelines with penalties and rewards
   b) Communicating policies and guidelines to the sales department

B. Evaluating

1. Being able to measure the sales effort as to efficiency through sales tracking

2. Keep accurate records on individual productivity in the sales force.

   a) Grosses
   b) Turns
   c) Closing ratios
   d) F&I production
   e) Demonstrations/presentations
   f) Follow-up
   g) Units... New and used

3. Establish the norm

   a) Measure and analyze each individual's production

4. Make evaluations known to the Sales Professional

   a) Create work and improvement programs for the group and for the individual

Planning Evaluating Coordinating, and Organizing

C. COORDINATING

Coordination is making sure the departments work together. Every department must work in cooperation and harmony with each other.

A manager has a keen awareness of the overall operation of the dealership, and the interaction of other departments. Create a keen awareness of the overall operation of the dealership and how every department must interact with one another

1. Create a spirit of teamwork and inter- departmental cooperation

2. Scheduling, quality time off

   a) Attention to high-traffic periods

3. Departmental profit integrity, respect

D. ORGANIZING

1. Setting up programs to insure the sales effort

   a) Determining a uniform sales system for the dealership
   b) Adjusting and monitoring compensation plans
   c) Procedures for handling customer relation's problems
   d) Training the sales force
   e) Install sales tracking system
   f) Meetings and scheduling
   g) Coordinating promotions and advertising and communicating to the sales force
   h) Delivery procedures, Inventory display/showroom displays/factory programs
   i) Keeping necessary records and analysis

2. Time management

   a) Working priorities
   b) Crisis management
   c) Single-minded ...single direction...no interruption of
      the sale

3. Management meetings and communication

4. Work programs to reduce non-applied time

CHOKING THE SALES EFFORT

I have often seen managers who were so bogged down with trivial paperwork and peripheral duties that they didn't have the time to dedicate the proper attention to directing the sales effort. The 'Sales Effort' is the primary job description of a sales manager. A dealer should have enough 'Clerical Support Employees' to remove duties from the sales manager's job that become a distraction and takes away attention to *'The Sales Effort'*.

HYPER AWARENESS

A Sales Manager should be aware of every opportunity to do business, as that opportunity happens, in real time. You need to be aware of the activities of every Sales Professional, every deal in progress, and where customers are physically, in the showroom or on the lot. You need to know what appointments are scheduled and what 'No Shows' you need to follow up with. The best Sales Managers have developed a keen sense of 'Hyper Awareness'. It is the quality that separates You from the average.

Timing and training are key elements in a successful sales operation. Nothing should bog a sales manager down or distract their attention from the number one priority, to get the car in the street. Dealers, be sure to give the manager enough clerical and support employees to get the job done without overloading him/her with clerk work.

Today's sales manager must be a diplomat and an ambassador of goodwill for the dealership and the product. The retail automobile industry will no longer tolerate the gypsies, tramps, and thieves that inhabited our showrooms not so long ago. The age of consumerism is upon us, and the retail automobile industry is working overtime at cleaning up their act. Without exception, every major manufacturer is very aware of customer satisfaction and legal compliance.

You Never Need to Lie, Cheat, Sneak, Steal or Deceive to Sell Cars

Jim can proudly say that he built a record-setting resume based on integrity and honesty. He is one of the few Nationally Recognized trainers and consultants with a published resume'. **http://www. ZieglerSuperSystems.com/about-Jim**

Jim Ziegler has always said, *"If You are a Criminal, We Need to Run You Out of The Car Business"*. This policy is not new, Ziegler has said this in speeches, seminars, magazine articles and textbooks, in writing dating back to the 1980's.

NEGOTIATION

Part of this course and part of the duties of the sales manager is the art of negotiation. Consider this is a give and take interaction between the Sales Professional and the consumer. Regardless of what they say, everybody loves to negotiate.

Negotiation, by its very nature, is stressful and emotional. Since negotiation is a mental combat between us and our customers, it is important to create a good feeling that lets everyone win and feel good about the outcome. It is a 'Chess Game'

Some of the techniques taught in this course are very sophisticated, applied psychology's, that measurably stack the deck on the side of the professional who practices his/her trade every day of their lives.

It is important to remember to treat your customers in such a way that makes the experience of buying their new car (or newer car) an adventure. This should be an exciting memorable occasion for them. What a shame that many Sales Professionals and managers have lost the magic.

All too many of us drudge through a day-to-day routine because we have come to think of automobile sales as just negotiating the numbers instead of selling the magic.

This course of study is all about the complexities and responsibilities of the position of sales manager in the current retail automobile sales environment.

It is a serious effort to improve your abilities to perform the duties of the job. Before we proceed, take some time, and think about what you are here to learn. Think about what you expect to learn and how you expect to improve in your profession. Make a commitment to take new techniques and methods back to your dealership and make immediate changes.

This seminar is presented in a forum format, which means that you are expected to participate and contribute to the group. At such times, please listen to and learn from the experiences of others.

HIRING, FIRING, TRAINING AND PROMOTING

Hiring, firing, training, and promoting are the interpersonal skills that a good Sales Manager needs to develop to have a competent, balanced sales force.

When you start thinking about adding new people to the sales force it is necessary to spend a little time analyzing exactly what you want and where you are going to find these people. Many inexperienced sales managers wait and only hire new people when there is a crisis situation, and they are under extreme pressure to hire immediately. In a well-balanced dealership the sales force is constantly turning over and churning at the bottom. What we mean by this is that the low producers are constantly being replaced by new personnel. Upgrading the quality of the sales force is a sound management objective; it is also a constant and continuing process.

Unfortunately, most dealerships terminate an employee only when there is an explosive incident or situation. Performance-generated turnover is necessary. Under performers and bad attitudes cannot remain employed by your dealership should be totally 100% 'Performance Based'.

As a matter of fact, Ziegler philosophy is that a Sales Department must be totally 'Performance-based'.

a) Performance based pay plans
b) Performance based promotion
c) Performance based termination

Every dealership has guidelines for hiring and terminating an employee. Once you realize that employee is never going to make it, then you need to put the wheels in motion for termination within your dealership's policy.

Now, It's not socially correct, but everything about the 'Old Jim Ziegler' doesn't fall within the guidelines of gentile Social Correctness. 35 years ago when Jim Ziegler was managing dealerships, I used to say (often) that there are 4 'E's' to Zieglerism …

a) Evaluate
b) Educate
c) Elevate
d) or Exterminate

The only reason I mention here in this more modernized text is to put it in perspective.

What I meant then, that still stands true today, is that a Sales Manager must first 'Evaluate' every employee regularly. Too many of us put too much value purely on the numbers, And, the stats are important, But; that's Not the total picture. It's not totally about how many units they've got out, or their closing ratio. Those things are certainly important, but 'Accountability' is also a factor.

Through the years, Ziegler has been known to terminate a man or woman selling 25 units a month because they were disruptive and caused problems. In some cases they had a bad attitude. In my world, a 'Bad Attitude' is grounds for termination, regardless of production. Too many Managers hang on to 'Bad Employees' who caused problems and dissention among other Sales Pros. You have to consider the good of the entire team and the good of the 'Selling Effort'.

Termination of employment is never an option until you have fully Evaluated their strengths and weaknesses and determined what training programs you've instituted. You cannot hold an employee, a Sales Pro, to your standards until you have thoroughly trained them.

'Training' is not solely about 'How to Sell a Car'. Have You trained your employees on what is expected of them? What are the mandatory duties of a professional Salesperson in this organization? So, in my thinking as a Manager, 'Training' is the 'Education part of the 4 E's of Zieglerism.

The 'Elevate' part of the equation means that Your Goal is to bring that person up to our standards. Not only that, but we should be elevating every man and woman in their profession. It is Not always possible to promote employees' positions. Some Dealerships are too small and there are No Management promotion opportunities. Other dealerships just don't have an opening right now. Whatever the case, we must never allow employees to feel they are in a dead-end job.

Years ago I created multi-layered pay plans with several levels.

a) Entry Level
b) Professional Level
c) Executive Level
d) Master Level

Each of the 4 Levels of the Pay Plan had requirements to achieve that level, and the Sales Pro had to maintain that level of performance 2 out of every 3 rolling months to stay at that level. Unless the Sales Pro had a vacation or an event in their life, they were expected to perform at that level to be promoted or kicked back to the previous level.

Every level of the pay plan had an increase in commission percentages and benefits, including a full-time assistant at the Master Level (This assistant later became a Sales Pro themselves).

Every Dealership that elected to use this pay plan, customized it to fit their situation, their size, and their culture.

The reason for this type of pay plan is simple, it never leaves the Salespersons feeling there is no possibility for advancement or promotion.

Occasionally, a dealership may terminate an employee because of lack of production. In the most desirable situation, a competent sales manager will systematically and regularly keep replacing and upgrading personnel who are at the bottom of acceptable performance levels, constantly upgrading the caliber of the sales force.

management-generated turnover is a constant process

It is almost always a certainty that many underperformers have negative attitudes, poor self-esteem, poor work habits, resentment of authority, or any number of negative traits that will pull the rest of the sales force down to that level.

Once we've decided that we are not going to hang on to Salespersons, or other Variable Department Employees (BDC), where do we find the winners that we want to become part of our team?

There is a strong possibility that the better applicants are not in the car business at all. Many modern-thinking managers are turning toward hiring people with no automobile sales experience whatsoever. The thinking here is that they would rather have someone who is trainable and willing to learn as opposed to someone who is hardened and indifferent to learning new concepts, ideas, and systems.

MANAGEMENT GENERATED TURNOVER

As we get into the concept of management-generated turnover, terminating employees becomes less an emotional experience and more a part of the plan. It is important to let the employees know that a certain performance level is expected, and that certain work ethics are demanded. You do this in writing. A written performance guideline is essential in a well-run dealership. When an employee's production falls below an acceptable level, the sales manager needs to counsel with the Sales Professional about his/her performance and what is expected of them.

A WRITTEN RECORD THAT YOU COUNSELED WITH THEM

In most states wrongful termination cases state that you must have a written record that you counseled with the employee and gave them a plan for improvement, including 'written warnings'. It is important that this policy is uniform, and the same standards are applied to everyone.

You want the employee to know that you'd rather find a way to keep them on the team than to lose them. You also want to make it clear that if their performance doesn't improve you will replace them.

Management-generated turnover insures your sales force will meet the high standards that you not only demand but expect them to maintain. As a sales manager you can never allow yourself to become too close to your employees. Hiring and firing are logical decisions because it's best for the dealership. You must be able to terminate any employee without guilt or intimidation.

HIRING

If the better-quality applicants are not working in the car business, what type of people are we looking for?

There are certain trades and people-oriented professions that are natural crossovers to become automobile Sales Professionals. Some of the best sales applicants I've seen have come from the food service and hospitality business. Yes, I'm talking about waiters and waitresses. People in these professions are used to longer hours and evening work and they're "people-oriented". The same personality type that is successful in food service is usually very easily suited to automobile sales.

Certain types of retail Sales Professionals, especially big-ticket department store types, are well suited to crossover into car sales. The possibilities here are endless if you just evaluate what you are really looking for and hire logically instead of emotionally. You are looking for people who are aggressive and assertive as well as amiable.

When you are thinking about a person as a Sales Professional in our business, it is important to determine if they have the drive to succeed. What motivates them? I am always aware of whether or not they are asking too many questions about secure income and guaranteed benefits. The last thing you need in a Sales Professional is a "welfare mentality" that demands that the job will take care of them whether they produce or not. Look for the hungry, aggressive, self-reliant applicant with the look in their eye that says they believe in themselves.

With women becoming a larger factor in decision-making in regard to car sales, it is logical that more and more women will be entering the industry as Sales Professionals. As automobile Sales Professionals, women are generally more detail-oriented, and are perceived to be more trustworthy by other women. A good sales manager will balance his/her sales force with a good representation of women.

When interviewing an applicant, you are looking for that certain chemistry...that right personality type that will fit in with your team. You are also looking for the negatives that would cause you not to hire this applicant. The obvious things to be aware of would-be things like dishonesty, alcohol or drug use, chronic absentee, bad driving record, tendency to steal, etc.

HIRING (CONT)

ALWAYS TEST FOR DRUG ABUSE WHEN IT IS LEGAL

Good managers and dealers have regular drug testing for all employees...no exceptions. (Check with the company attorney for guidelines)

Always make the calls. Sometimes, the dealer wants the HR Department to check out the applicants. BUT, if it's not against the rules, a good manager might want to do some checking on your own.

You might say, *"Hey Ziegler, we have an HR Department to do that"*

If the applicant says they are working somewhere and you are not able to check that reference, call anyway and verify that they do actually work there. You can do this without giving them away to their current employer. Many times you will find out that the applicant has actually been fired and that they no longer work there but they said they did just so you wouldn't be able to check that reference.

Recruiting new Sales Professionals is easy once you deviate from the beaten paths. The most obvious recruits are all around you every day.

Rather than spend money advertising for applicants, why not pay your Sales Professionals to recruit new applicants.

Think about it. Doesn't it make sense that your current producers know some people who are very much like themselves? If you are always aware of the people who are all around you most of the time, you'll stumble across some very qualified applicants every day. Don't be embarrassed to ask the Sales Professional at the department store if they've ever considered changing professions ... The waiter at the restaurant...perfect!

When staffing your sales force, it is important that the team is balanced in regard to personalities. There is always room for one more good sales applicant on the sales force. What we mean by this is that you should never turn away an applicant that you want to hire. If you hire one too many, the sales force will adjust and level itself out with the weakest link leaving voluntarily.

The correct number of Sales Professionals for any dealership has always been a mathematical mystery. Some schools of thought lean toward hiring one Sales Professional for every eight units you plan to sell. Others say that it is best to hire one Sales Professional for every three customers who come through the showroom on any average day.

Regardless of what school of thought you subscribe to; it is never a crime to hire too many Sales Professionals. Too few Sales Professionals, however, will cost you both unit sales and gross profits.

HOW MANY SALES PROFESSIONALS

Staffing is one of the things necessary to grow a dealership to its full potential.

Too few Sales Professionals is worse than having too many. Every dealership that I've grown to the Big Numbers, with almost no exceptions, we had to increase the number of Sales Professionals. In my experience, most dealerships are understaffed to meet their potential numbers.

In today's dealerships traffic comes from many different directions and sources. If your dealership has a BDC, it is their responsibility to turn 'Leads into 'Shows'.

Whether a customer comes to the dealership through text, phone, internet lead, or walk-in; the number of opportunities determines how many Sales Professionals and BDC staff you'll need. Regardless, somebody has to set the appointment and turn that 'Lead' into an 'Appointment' that 'Shows'. In other words, the number of opportunities dictates how many Sales Professionals we need.

If each Sales Professional has fewer opportunities (ups), then they will work the ones they have harder and smarter. Remember, anytime you have more Sales Professionals on the floor than necessary. The situation will correct itself.

Once again, one of the Sales Professionals' main jobs is to set appointments. Many opportunities should be generated by the CRM. Unfortunately, Sales Professionals and managers have lost the art of prospecting. The best Sales Professionals in our business, selling 150-200 units a month, have developed their own processes for prospecting and generating their own business.

Unfortunately, Sales Pros selling more than 100 units a month are extremely rare, and regardless of what you've heard, the average Sales Pro sells 8 units a month. Of course we don't want to be 'Average' but you have to plan staffing on an 8 unit average.

SO, if I project the dealership has a realistic potential to sell 160 units a month, then I nee to have 20 Sales Pros on staff. This formula has never failed me when growing a dealership to its maximum potential.

Too few Sales Pros will never produce the numbers, and they have a tendency to waste opportunities when they have too many opportunities. It is a sure sign that you are understaffed when there are too many Sales Pros selling more than 20 units a month each. Remember this, most salespeople average 8 units, so, when you artificially supply such an abundance of opportunities (ups) that everyone can sell 20 units, then; you're wasting up because they are not dear enough to them.

Regardless of how the customer comes into the dealership, whether they are an internet lead, appointment or just a walkup customer; when my Sales Pros average more than 3 opportunities a day, face to face on the lot customers, then I need more Salespersons.

Of course I will still have some exceptional people that will still speak to 4, or 5, or even 6 customers a day, but the average over the entire sales force averages 3 customers per Sales Pro per day. That is when we need more Sales Pros.

Think about it, if they are averaging 3 opportunities a day, that would 75 face-to-face customers every month. Excuse me! When a Sales Professional can't make a great living with 75 opportunities a month, then we have a severe problem.

ZIEGLER ON ZOOM: I have an excellent two-hour course I teach on prospecting for dealerships via Zoom broadcasts. There is nobody in the world who knows more about prospecting than me. I can walk out of any dealership in the world, and providing it is good weather, not a Sunday, and not a holiday, I can generate a lead from out of any community and deliver a car to a stranger before the sun sets.

Don't believe all of the hype, not all customers submit a lead or come in on the phone, text, or internet. There is still a considerable number of prospects that still walk on the lot and did Not come in through the internet.

A sales manager's job is to verify the leads coming from the BDC and the Sales Professionals. Sometimes, the BDC Director is verifying the appointments and pushing verified appointments to the sales manager through the CRM or with paper reports. Training is ongoing, and starts with a training session in every sales meeting

Most dealerships hire a new applicant and then throw them in a room by themselves for several days with a stack of videotapes about the product and the different models and their features.

A new applicant gets very little training on the sales system of the dealership and the sales philosophy of the store. As the sales manager it is important that you supervise very new Sales Professional's orientation and initial training. A couple of hours every morning on Sales Procedures and product presentation with each new applicant.

The ongoing training process will elevate some of your Sales Professionals to a performance level that indicates that they are ready for more responsibility. Every successful dealership should be set up in a way that every employee believes that their position is not a dead-end job.

The most competent Sales Professionals could be given backup management duties such as training director, assistant manager, F&I backup, closer positions, etc...

PRODUCTIVE SALES MEETINGS

A productive sales meeting schedule would require a sales meeting every morning, before work at eight-thirty, with all of the Sales Professionals and managers who are scheduled to be on shift that morning.

A sales meeting with the entire assembled sales force and management team should be held at least twice a week. I always preferred Saturday morning and Wednesday morning.

Regardless of When You Prefer to Have Sales Meetings, One Thing I Would Always Recommend is a Meeting On Saturday Morning

The morning Sales Meeting lasts no more than 30 minutes. It is a business meeting with the Sales Pros to discuss appointments, Be-Backs, Deals that need attention. Hopefully, the Sales Manager has all of this logged in the CRM.

Sales meetings should be in a two-part format, half training, and half business

The training half of the meeting should be limited to one-half hour and conducted by different managers, in rotation, on varied subjects. This includes sessions with the used car manager, the F&I manager, new car manager, general sales manager, and maybe even the office manager. It is important that the training sessions are active and that the Sales Professionals be tested on what they absorbed. Training topics range from product presentation techniques to sessions on how to properly introduce a customer to the F&I manager.

The business half of the meeting is a review of deals working and deliveries scheduled for today. The managers ask the Sales Professionals if they need assistance on any deals and they review the Sales Professionals work plan for the day

Review how many appointments (manager or BDC Director verifies appointments)

a) Do you have deals working
b) Where do you plan to get your new business from?
c) Assignment of leads

After every sales meeting, managers should meet and discuss plans to divide the callback assignments of customers who were in the dealership yesterday but didn't buy and verify Sales Pro's appointments.

SALES PROFESSIONAL DEVELOPMENT AND TRAINING

Every Dealership I ever worked for or worked with always had an organized training regimen. In the larger stores we even had an employee who was designated as the Training Director. That was their full-time job, organizing sales training and even assigning other managers to teach certain subjects.

These classes included role-play walk-arounds on new product, or fresh trade-in off-brand used cars and trucks. When was the last time you had the Used Car Manager take the Sales Pros for a tour of the pre-owned inventory?

When was the last time you had the Sales Pros role play working a deal? In other words, You described a scenario and wrote the numbers on a white board, projector, or a flip chart, and told the Sales Pros to role play this deal? Have them in groups of three or four, and ask them … *"How would you work this deal?"* Maybe, it's the difficult deal we had yesterday. Real figures, how would you have handled that deal in the role play?

All Managers take turns at 'training'. The General Sales Manager might be really good at training, but we actually need all of the managers to participate in training. That way it develops teamwork and respect of the Sales Pros for the authority of the management.

    a) Role play walkarounds on New and Used Cars
    b) Role play working deals with different situations

1. The upside-down trade-in deal
2. The no trade-in deal
3. The cash customer
4. How to get the down payment deal
5. How to T.O. to F&I, taught by the F&I Manager
6. Product knowledge certifications, videos, and tests

7. We want all Sales Professionals certified on all products, so we supervise the training videos and testing

   c) Who's responsible for sales training? Most Dealerships are not large enough to have a fulltime Training Director, so who is the Manager that accepts responsibility for scheduling training? If he/she doesn't get cooperation, then the GSM or GM needs to enforce the training program. It's that important. A trained team becomes Seal Team 6, highly professional and respected.
   d) Experienced Sales Pros are Not excused from the training. Stop assuming they know everything.

MINIMUM RESPONSIBILITIES OF A SALES PROFESSIONAL

A Sales Professional will show up on time, every day, well-groomed and well-dressed, with a good attitude, ready to do business.

A Sales Professional will follow up regularly with all previously sold customers and all "adopted customers". Every customer contact starts with three human interest (CSI) oriented questions before you discuss other business

a) Use video walkarounds

b) Video lead response with customers

> A Sales Professional will learn to use the CRM to set appointments, follow up with previous customers, record notes about conversations, and set reminders about future tasks and appointments. In the CRM, he/she will record the name, address, email, and phone numbers of every prospect they speak to in a timely manner with attention to detail and accuracy.

> The CRM is the heartbeat of the Sales Effort. Everything is recorded and all actions go through the CRM.

a) We're working the deal through the CRM OR maybe (in some dealerships) through the Digital Retailing tools.

> Demonstrate every customer and tour the dealership before they attempt to write-up a deal

> Any prospect that was not closed, sold, and/or delivered on the first visit must be followed up within twenty-four hours of their initial visit, and a thank you email, or video follow-up should be generated.

> 100% of all prospects talked to by a Sales Professional must be turned over (introduced) to a manager before they leave the dealership. A Manager will speak to every customer a Sales

Pro interacts with on the lot or in the showroom, even if it is a 'Service Department Customer'. Managers do NOT refuse to take a T.O.

A Sales Professional will attempt to write up every prospect that demonstrates an automobile

A Sales Professional must always know their individual closing ratio and their average gross per deal and where they stand in relation to their monthly forecast

THE ROAD TO THE SALE SELLING SYSTEM

Every dealership must have an established road to the sale, a step-by-step selling procedure...a selling system that must be followed, without exception, from the first moment that a Sales Professional approaches the prospect through the follow-up after the sale.

In one form or another, the road to the sale has been around since there were franchised dealerships and organized sales departments.

The reason that the road to the sale has endured the decades is because it's the only intelligent way to sell automobiles.

As I mentioned previously, The Road to the Sale didn't Die, we just incorporated the Internet and technology into it. Digital Retail never happened as far as the majority of customers totally buying their cars online, but it can be a tremendously good desking tool, especially if you're working tools on the phone or internet.

Try as they may, no one has ever successfully re-invented the basics of the retail automobile Sales Process.

The road to the sale is not a way to sell cars...it is the way to sell cars.

There are no shortcuts on the road to the sale. A Sales Professional must take his prospect through every step in the process, never skipping a step ...never deviating from the format. Every step of the road to the sale must be done in order ...exactly the way it is designed... No exceptions accepted.

Management's problem is that Sales Professionals, as they become more experienced, become experts in their own minds. They feel they are too good to have to stick with these basics. More often than not, it is the experienced Sales Professionals short- cutting the road to the sale and skipping important steps, not the brand-new Sales Professionals as one might reasonably expect to be the case. How many times have we seen a supposedly experienced professional trying to close the deal with a prospect that hasn't even driven the automobile? Talking figures and negotiating on the parking lot?

When a Sales Professional begins to feel that they're such an expert that they feel they no longer need the road to the sale, that's when they start to lose sales and their grosses decline.

EXPERTISE IS A TERRIBLE DISEASE

One of the most horrible diseases a Sales Professional could catch is a bad case of *"expertise"*.

When management doesn't require Sales Professionals to follow the road to the sale...or even worse than that...when management isn't even aware of whether or not their Sales Professionals are following the road to the sale, the quality of the sales effort suffers. This is the "Old School Road to the Sale", the way it's been for many decades. The evolution of the Internet, and technology, with the introduction of Digital Retailing has changed the steps, but still, in some form, we do all of them.

The number one responsibility of any sales manager is the day-to-day, one-on-one supervision of his/her Sales Professionals

1. Meet and Greet the Customer

2. Establish Common Ground

3. Select a Vehicle

4. Present the Vehicle

5. Demonstrate the Vehicle

6. Inspect (and Drive) the Vehicle

7. Tour the Dealership

8. Write and Negotiate the Deal

9. Turnover to F&I With a Quality T.O.

10. Deliver the Car

11. Follow Up With the Customer

This eleven-step selling system is the difference between success and failure in any dealership. It is the difference between a disorganized group of entrepreneurs, self-managed, each doing his/her own thing, and a highly polished professional sales organization. There are many subtle variations of the road to the sale format with different twists, but the essence of all the variations is basically the same.

The road to the sale must be learned by every Sales Professional, backwards and forwards, constantly drilled and retaught. Management must demand that the steps be followed to the letter. **This is not an option; it is the way we do business. Every Sales Professional will follow this format...period.**

SALES DESK CONTROL

To maximize efficiency in unit sales and in gross profits, it is absolutely necessary that every dealership has a workable sales system.

A modern retail automobile dealership without an organized selling system is a lost puppy on the center line of an interstate highway at rush hour.

The sales system revolves around the sales control desk. All sales strategy and all Sales Procedure are directed by the manager on the desk. It is extremely important that the manager on the desk is uninterrupted by non-sales-related activities while he/she is working deals. The desk manager must always be available and not distracted by clerical duties or telephone calls. He/she must be aware and in control of every deal in progress.

It is extremely important that the sales desk is regarded as a place where business takes place. Any Sales Professionals without specific business at the desk should not be hanging around. The manager at the desk should have a reasonably good view of the lot and the sales area to increase his/her awareness of the flow of business.

The reason for the desk is to control and supervise the Sales Professionals as they work deals with your prospects. Without management, a Sales Professional will always take the easiest route to get the car delivered...or, at least, what they perceive to be the easiest route. By nature, Sales Professionals want to make the deal worse than they want to hold the gross. It is up to management to control, manage, coach, and supervise them through the sale. Part of the function of the desk is to slow the Sales Professionals down and to keep the progress of the sale orderly.

The sales system works the same way every time. There is no room for experimentation and there are no exceptions to the procedures outlined in the sales system. It is never acceptable to deviate from the system for any reason.

Never allow any Sales Professional to be exempt from having to follow the system.

The sales system is absolute; there are no shades of gray. One of the biggest reasons that sales systems lose their effectiveness is because people tamper with the system. This gradual erosion of the original system changes its character completely.

Never let anyone make even the slightest change in the system's procedures no matter how innocent or trivial it may_ seem.

At the sales desk, Sales Professionals bring their deals to the manager to get the deal started. The manager logs every deal and then tracks the prospect through the sale. A good desk manager is on top of everything that is happening. He/she will send the Sales Professional back in with the prospect with strategies and counterproposals. The desk manager will negotiate with the prospect through the Sales Professional. This is done with a series of proposals and counterproposals. Using a series of bright colored felt markers, the manager will rewrite the offers until the original worksheet looks like a war zone.

Very early in the deal the manager will have a credit bureau pulled on every prospect at the earliest legal moment. Knowing who you're dealing with will guide the manager in formulating strategies.

Pull up a credit bureau report on every customer at the earliest legal moment...before you negotiate the deal

Once we have decided that this deal is going to be a spot delivery (courtesy delivery), the F&I manager and the Sales Professional go into the spot delivery mode. Everything starts to move very quickly and the sale's pace, the heartbeat of the sale, is speeded up. Spot deliver every possible deal...every time. Get your Sales Professionals thinking spot delivery... Think urgency!

DESK CONTROL

All Deals Start at the Desk

The desk manager will record the customer in the CRM as soon as we are aware they're here.

a) Which Sales Pro they're with?
b) What time did we first see them?
c) What is the physical description of the customer(s), we'll substitute that with their name later

No interruptions or non-sales related activities at the desk . Sales Professionals without business at the sales desk should not be hanging around. No one should be watching or commenting as I am working on another person's deal. I don't need a wanna-be manager coaching me how to work a deal.

If people Do Not have business at the sales desk, the manager needs to find something else for them to do.

Every deal must have a completely filled out worksheet, or all of the required information, in the CRM before the desk manager will start the deal.

Did we scan their driver's license?
Pull a credit bureau report at the earliest legal moment?
No Sales Professionals to sell from inventory cards or invoices
Desk manager determines when to appraise trade
All appraisals are sealed, and the ACV of the Trade-in is unknown to the Sales Pro while the deal is working.
This is so the Sales Pro doesn't manage their own deal. The ACV is really the only number they don't know.

Every deal must have a good faith retainer (deposit) or a partial payment before management will consider the prospect's counteroffer. If the Sales Professional comes to the desk without the money, send them back to the prospect

Without good faith money, the deal stops. Do not negotiate without the money. Only management can start the deal back up without the money

No Sales Professional may release a prospect without management permission This is a strict rule with the best Sales Managers. All prospects are T.O.ed (Introduced) to management while the deal is still makeable before the salesperson has said goodbye. I would prefer the customers are sitting down and relaxed.

First Touch: Questions that the Sales Desk Manager may ask the Sales Professional when he/she first brings the deal to the sales desk

a) Have they driven the automobile?
b) The desk manager will be doubly sure that the customer has driven the car and will buy it if figures are agreeable
c) Did you scan their driver's licenses, both of them?
d) Have You discussed figures with them?
e) Will they own the automobile NOW if everything is agreeable?
f) Do you think we have a sale?
g) Will we be adding any equipment to the car?
h) Is all of the information in the CRM?
i) Will we be making any repairs, or are they expecting any recon? (Used cars)
j) Are all of the decision makers present?
k) Are the customers in your office?
l) Are they sitting down?
m) Do you have them under control?
n) What do the customers think you're doing right now?
o) What are you going to say to them when you go back in?
p) Where do you think we're at in this deal?
q) What would you like me to do next?
r) Did you walk-around the trade-in?
s) Describe the trade-in to me?
t) Is this car ready for spot delivery?

THE DEAL STARTS AND FINISHES IN THE CRM

When the deal first shows up at the sales desk, the manager knows how long the Sales Pro has been with the customers. That information should be in the CRM because a manager first entered it when we first became aware of the Sales Pro with the customer. It might just be a description of the customer, but now we know their name, BUT, most importantly, they didn't fall through the cracks. The desk manager will be sure that the Sales Professional has not taken any shortcuts in the "road to the sale" process.

What if I have a description of the customer in my CRM, say that it says, "Lady in blue dress with Jonathan at 10:20 AM", but here comes Jonathan with no customer at 1:00 PM. I know I never spoke to the lady in the blue dress, and I ask the other managers if they did. Uh-oh, it appears that Jonathan released that customer with no manager introduction (No T.O.). We have a problem we'll be discussing with Jonathan.

Generally, if the deal has not been started by the BDC, or on the Internet, or digital retail tool; with a trade-in, including the demo drive, I am expecting that the Sales Pro has been with the customer 45 minutes by the time they bring the deal to the sales desk. That is 'If' they've done their job properly.

Timing is the heartbeat of the deal. As an experienced manager, you will learn instinctively when the deal is bogging down and you're losing the 'heartbeat'. When you need to slow down or speed up the process. You'll know when you need to stop the deal and go in to meet the customers yourself.

You also feel when the Sales Pro has skipped steps or taken shortcuts, or there's something they're not telling you.

If the customer will not give the Sales Professional a tentative commitment, the manager must go in on the deal. Do not continue to give the customer discounts if they won't counteroffer to your initial proposal. There's really no reason to negotiate against yourself if the customer will not commit that they would consider owning the automobile at some figure.

My philosophy is to never let the customer leave the dealership with my lowest figure. Let them leave with a high figure. Then work feverishly to get them back. Let's face it, if you let them leave and they go to another dealership, they'll beat your number no matter how low it is. I'd rather try to get them back and have room to work. If they buy elsewhere, I really don't want to ruin somebody else's deal at the competition, they deserve to have a good life and make some money. I want to keep the perceived value of my product up in the market.

THE DESK MANAGER

The desk manager will be sure that the Sales Professional has not taken any shortcuts in the "road to the sale" procedure.

The desk manager will be doubly sure that the customer has driven the car and will buy it if figures are agreeable

The desk manager should not start a deal if the customer will not commit that they would consider owning the automobile at some figure

If the customer will not give the Sales Professional a tentative Commitment, the manager must go in on the deal.

The desk manager does not give out shopping figures under any circumstances. If the customer wants the figures but will not consider owning the vehicle at any figure, we will not give them any figures.

FINANCE

No salesman should quote a rate, or a payment, an interest rate, or an approximate payment to a customer. Only a manager may sell finance

Anytime a Sales Professional has sold finance, the finance manager and the sales manager should have a meeting with that Sales Professional right away

If a Sales Professional quotes a rate or a payment to a customer, or prices an extended warranty, or discusses credit insurance with the customer that is considered selling finance. Only a manager should sell finance. Sales Professionals who sell finance without management supervision and authorization have seriously violated the policy of the dealership.

The payment is an invoice. Anyone who quotes a payment is responsible for the profitability of the F&I department on that deal. A manager who strips out a payment...for any reason ...has sabotaged the F&I department's opportunity to make a profit on that deal.

Whoever quotes the payment is responsible for the F&I profit

There is never a need to throw in an extended service contract to be included at no charge in the deal during the sale or any of the F&I products for that matter.

THE DESK MANAGER CONTROLS THE SALE

When a desk manager is working the deal with the Sales Professional it is important that we never lose sight of the fact that although the Sales Professional's input is important, we are the manager, and we are in control of the deal.

A Sales Professional wants the deal more than they want the gross

Never let a weak Sales Professional sell you into taking a weak deal when you don't have to. When the negotiation process begins, it is the desk manager's role to be the coach that sends the Sales Professional in with the plays, not to be the quarterback who runs every play him/herself. The manager needs to negotiate through the Sales Professional and needs to stay out of the deal, away from the customer, until the negotiations break down or the customer starts to walk.

Once the manager sends the Sales Professional to the customer with the initial proposal, it is the Sales Professional's job to get the prospect's **commitment** or the prospect's counter proposal. This is one area where many sales departments tend to get weak and give up the gross.

All too many of your Sales Professionals think it is their job to go in with the customer and come back with a counterproposal.

"That's all wrong" ...your Sales Professionals need to get the Attitude that they are going in there to sell the customer on your original offer, not to get a counteroffer. Your Sales Professionals know the routine because this is the way you've trained them.

Once the prospect has made a commitment or a counterproposal the Sales Professional must get the money. We're talking about getting the prospect's down payment, all of it, or getting the prospect's partial payment or good faith retainer. Whatever the case, the Sales Professional should not return to the sales desk without the money.

If the Sales Professional brings the counteroffer to the desk without the money, do not work the deal...send them back to the prospect to get the money. Until we have the money, the deal is stopped... at a standstill. Do not work the prospect's offer without the money.

GET THE MONEY (CONT)

This is the one single most point in the negotiation process where managers become weak. Never allow Sales Professionals to get in the habit of working deals without the money. Don't accept excuses...and don't make excuses yourself...

When the Sales Professional has gotten the prospect's commitment or counterproposal and the money, the manager makes still another counterproposal by writing over the worksheet with a bright colored felt-tip marker.

Before sending the Sales Professional back to the prospect, rehearse everything that he/she is going to say when they get there...word-for-word.

Keep the Sales Professional calm, positive and motivated during the negotiation. It is not necessary to explain or debate your decisions with the Sales Professional. If the Sales Professional argues with you, take control and be a manager. All too many Sales Professionals waste valuable salesmanship on a manager, trying to sell the manager that the deal can't be made, or the bump can't be done.

The deal should bump back and forth several times before you and the customer reach a common ground agreement. The more times you send the Sales Professional back, the better deal the customers perceive that they got.

It is very important that the manager goes in before the Sales Professional gets weak and commits to the customer.

If you sense the strain of the negotiation is wearing down your Sales Professional, get involved right away before they give the gross away. An inexperienced manager or a weak manager always gets involved after the Sales Professional has locked them out...or already committed to the customer.

CONTROLLING THE SALES FFORT

The average Sales Professional will always give up at least $700 more than they have to without supervision.

The manager must stay on top of the deal. In a trade-in situation, you might elect to start the deal without appraising the trade. Unless the BDC has already committed to the numbers, I will almost always start the first set of figures I send in with a guess on the trade-in ACV, unless there is a really glaring situation, like major body damage or the customer has told the Sales Pro something about the car that might make me stop the deal and get an appraisal.

Based on the accurate description that your salesperson has given you; you have a pretty good idea what you're dealing with in trade value. Assume the car is average book or less. Use a hypothetical figure based on a formal appraisal later. When you get to the point in the negotiation where a formal appraisal is required, send the salesperson to the used car appraiser to get the appraisal.

Never allow the salesperson to know the appraisal (acv) while the deal is in progress.

The Sales Professional never sees the figure until the deal is over. Many dealerships using this system prefer to seal the appraisals in an envelope. When Sales Professionals are working blind with the figures you send in with them to the prospect, the grosses will usually be considerably higher.

NEVER ever allow salespeople to have access invoices or invoice quoted in the CRM. The numbers belong to management.

The actual cost of the car is manager's domain. The Sales Professionals are too close to the deals emotionally to be responsible knowing the cost figures. Once Sales Professionals learn what you will accept as an acceptable deal, you will lose gross on every deal they work until you regain control.

Every sales manager has to constantly be aware when his people start self-managing their deals.

When Sales Professionals manage themselves, the manager loses control of the sales effort, and he/she loses respect, command, and authority.

No Sales Professional can be above the system and no Sales Professional is above being managed by the managers.

Even if we're talking about the top Sales Professional in the dealership, either they are a part of the team, on the program just like everyone else, or you have a serious problem.

The absolute worst mistake I have ever seen a dealer make is when the dealer or the general manager puts a single Sales Professional outside of management control. No matter how good a Sales Pro is, when they are Not accountable to Sales managers, you'll have disruption and problems with the entire team.

When this happens, you create a spoiled brat who ultimately contaminates and ruins the rest of the sales force and destroys management authority.

I've heard dealers say... ***"Dammit Jim, I can't fire the man/ woman! They're selling sells 20 cars a month!"***

My answer has always been the same... Ziegler says, ***"Fire their ass and replace them with three 'Green Peas', one that sells ten and two that sell five.***

So, all humor aside, regardless of their sales, I'd fire prefer to fire a bad attitude. No dealership can be held hostage by the whims of an out-of-control, spoiled brat, no matter how good they are. Remember, Sales Manager is a title of dignity, authority, and respect. I earned that title, and I will Not be disrespected.

Throughout the negotiation the desk manager is there to coach and assist as well as direct the sales effort. I am in charge.

The pitfalls and traps that the desk manager might fall into all revolve around losing control of the Sales Process during the negotiation. The negotiation is an absolute process. A procedure that must be done the same way every time with precision, training, and enthusiasm. The reason that procedures work is because there is no tolerance for deviation.

NEGOTIATING THE DEAL

The retail automobile business is one of the last businesses in the world where people still haggle and negotiate the price that they will pay for a retail product.

No matter what type of process your dealership uses, the customers still expect to negotiate. Even in a 'One Price' or 'No Haggle' dealership, they still expect us to negotiate, and most dealerships actually do. Regardless of your store's philosophy, the Manager Owns the Numbers.

Effective negotiators realize that it's your role in the sale to make as much profit as possible while still delivering the automobile. The customer's role in the negotiation is to pay you as little profit as possible.

a) All deals start at the desk and the manager owns the numbers. Salespersons Do Not quote figures, approximate numbers, or *'Ball Park Figures'*. The deal is started by the desk manager after asking questions.

b) Even in an A-to-Z Dealership, where the managers (or coaches, or whatever we call them to disguise the fact they are managers) are not readily visible to the customers, even in that type of Sales Process, the manager is still authoring the numbers, or a range of numbers in the background.

c) The Sales Pro is thoroughly trained on the word tracks and Sales Processes. As a manager, we expect them to use the exact methods and processes they've been taught. That goes for managers as well.

Jim Ziegler has often said this Zieglerism, *"In the Car Business we don't have a 'Knowing' problem. We have a 'Doing' problem."*

What that means is our Sales Pros and our Managers have been thoroughly trained but that does not necessarily mean we're doing exactly what we were trained to do or to say.

As a General Sales Manager or General Manage/Dealer, I expect my managers to desk deals exactly the way they were taught, whatever our company policy and processes are. There are too many dealerships with four Sales Managers, all working deals a different way.

It is the desk manager's job to slow the sale down and to make the Sales Professional spend more time selling the features and benefits and demonstrating the automobile. Sales Professionals tend to rush into the negotiation stages of the sale far too quickly.

Personally, I have worked physically in 1000s of dealerships in 49 out of 50 states. Every dealership has slightly, or even dramatically, different ways they work deals. Truthfully, I don't care how you work deals at your store. I don't even claim my way is the best way for all dealerships. All I say is that you must have consistency in your processes, every manager working the same way and demanding the Sales Pros do it exactly the way they were taught.

The common misconception that many so-called professionals have is that negotiation involves only money. There are other factors to negotiate a deal other than money.

In the negotiation part of the sale it is important that the Sales Professional has not taken any shortcuts in the 'road to the sale presentation'. The first thing a good desk manager must do is determine whether or not the Sales Professional has sold the automobile before we start trying to justify a higher price.

Remember, a salesperson will always go for the easiest perceived route to get the car delivered.

The sales manager has to be aware of every deal in progress, in every stage of the deal. When the Sales Professional first brings the deal to the sales desk the desk manager must ask a series of calculated questions before he/she starts the deal into the negotiation process. Once the sales manager has a good feel for where the Sales Professional is at with the prospect and whether or not they are in control, then he/she starts the deal by giving the Sales Professional the starting figure to take back to the customer. At this point, the customer is either negotiating on trade allowance, discounts, or payments. In the end however, it's probably going to be all about the Payment and the Down Payment.

One quote that every Sales Manager needs to take to heart and repeat often in every sales meeting is

Nobody Walks Until the Man (Woman) Talks!

Jackie B. Cooper, legendary sales trainer, circa 1977

The words of Jackie B. Cooper still reflect upon the best Sales Managers in the car business. The Sales Manager – Desk Manager – Assistant Manager/Closer, no Sales Professional will release or say 'Good-Bye' to customer until they are introduced to a Manager. As a General Sales Manager, I will have a serious discussion with one of my managers that won't get off the desk and go speak with the customer. Any Manager that refuses to take a T.O. (Turnover, customer introduction) will not be a Manager much longer in my organization.

Truthfully, a Manager needs to touch every customer early before you are in 'Combat'. When that customer is introduced to me by a Sales Pro, they have already met me previously.

If it's legal in your state, and the dealership allows it, always think , 'Puppy Dog Close'.

Tell the customer that you'd like to send them home in the car they're considering and leave their trade-in here so we can have some professional buyers in our market come by and look at it to see if there's added allowance we can pay for their trade. This is a true statement by the way. I will shop their car.

Work the deal on trade allowance or discount

Working the deal based on payments_

The four-square/reactor procedure_

THE FOUR-SQUARE SELLING SYSTEM

The four-square, or reaction system, is a method by which a manager can control the deal through the Sales Professional using extremely close desk control. The primary philosophy of this type of sale is that a retail automobile sale is broken down to its four basic elements, which are...

1. Selling Price

2. Trade Allowance

3. Down Payment

4. Payment

Most dealerships today use either some variation of this method or a straight trade difference negotiation.

The whole idea of this method is for the manager to send the Sales Professional to the customer to present all four of these elements *at the* same time.

If the Sales Professionals or the managers are weak or poorly trained this system can be a disaster.

Personally, I have seen some of the highest imaginable gross profits, front and back, on this selling system.

A sales manager on the desk using this system must have control of the Sales Professional. A Sales Professional cannot be responsible with a payment since they are already emotionally involved with the customer. All payments and interest rates given to the customer are directed by management.

The figures come from the desk every time. A Sales Professional should never ask the customer what they would like to pay or what they want for their trade-in.

We don't want to know what the customer wants before we make our first offer to them.

This is the one area where most amateur sales managers mess up. Once a customer has told you what they want, they're locked into defending that for the rest of the sale. You usually end up trying to "raise the customer".

The basic theory behind the four-square/reaction system is that the customer is put into a posture of having to try to Bump or raise us instead of us hearing the customer's number (which is always too low) and then we have to 'Bump' them up.

Before we send the first set of figures into the customer, I prefer that the Sales Professional avoids all questions about what the customer says they want to pay and what deals they were offered elsewhere. I don't want a Sales Professional to let the customer get into a conversation about the figures some other dealer offered them.

Whatever figure the customer says the other dealer offered them is probably going to be a lie anyway. Nobody tells the truth about the deal they were offered elsewhere. If the customer insists on knowing all of the numbers at this point, all the Sales Pro says

… "Look, Mr. Customer, I'd rather that you not tell me what they offered you down the street at the other dealership. Let's wait until you see my manager's proposal. It might be a much better deal if my manager doesn't know what the other dealer offered you, so don't tell me now". (actually, this is better for us and for the customer)

WE DON'T WANT TO KNOW THE CUSTOMER'S NUMBER

The main reason that we don't want to know is that we don't want to have to counter offer against some other dealer's figures before we show the customers our full list price, with ACV for their trade-in, with an interest rate at the proper tier level they qualify for, including a 20% down-payment figure.

THE FOUR-SQUARE SELLING SYSTEM
(continued)

There is a big danger of Managers and Sales Pros getting weak here. When the manager starts the foursquare-worksheet, all of the blanks have been filled out except the four-squares. At that point the manager writes or prints out of the CRM …

Full list price plus adds in the first square

$500 range starting at ACV in the trade-in square

20% of the selling price in the down-payment square

And an accelerated equity payment of 48 months in the payment square.

(If there is no trade, use only three squares)

This is the point when many managers and most Sales Professionals can lose their nerve and blow the deal.

It is absolutely essential that every customer is given the opportunity to pay full list price, front and back. My attitude has always been that 'Full Price is a Fair Price'".

I Do Not believe we are cheating anyone selling our vehicles for all of the money, meaning MSRP or a reasonable markup on used vehicles. So, My second saying is, 'All the Money, All the Time'.

The four-square system is absolutely one of the best or it is absolutely one of the worst selling systems currently being used to sell automobiles. It is often misunderstood.

James A. Ziegler

THE FOUR-SQUARE SELLING SYSTEM
(continued)

Most dealerships using a four-square or reaction system are doing the system very badly. Most dealerships using a four-square system have terrible F&I numbers and weak to average grosses on the front.

This is 100% the sales manager's or desk manager's fault. The problem in most dealerships is that they are closing on the Payment instead of closing on the 'Down Payment.

One thing we learned from the inventory shortage and the Pandemic, is that customers will pay all of the money. Of course, Jim Ziegler has been saying that and proving that for more than 30 years. If every deal starts out at all of the money, full list, every time, it stands to reason we'll make better grosses, front and back.

As I have said repeatedly, there's never a need to lie, or cheat, deceive, or hide the figures. Everything we do can be done in a forthright, upfront, ethical and legally compliant disclosure.

It's true that the four-square system is a selling system that converts most of the customers to payment buyers. Many reputable surveys have shown that the majority of customers are actually payment buyers. In my personal experience with 1000s of dealerships and many 1000s of customers, I can tell you experientially, that is 100% true. So, my thinking is let's start with the payment and make the figures fit to what the customer agrees to.

There is no sense in negotiating a sales price, then a trade allowance, and coming to an agreement, only to find out that the customer can't afford the payment.

Think about it for a second. No matter how much you give a customer for their trade-in, or how much you discount the car, if the payment doesn't work for the customer, we don't have a deal.

THE FOUR-SQUARE SELLING SYSTEM
(continued)

If your dealership is on the four-square/reaction system of selling automobiles, chances are that someone is not handling the deals correctly. My experience has been that most managers in most dealerships are not responsible handling the payments. Usually the reason the deals start out on the first pass with a huge discount, or a low payment with 84 months on the first pass, or an over-allowance on the trade; the reason for all of those things is we over-qualified the customer. We found out too much about what they wanted to pay before we showed them our figures.

Remember I said earlier, I don't want to know what they want to pay until they've seen our numbers first. One of the stupidest questions a Sales Pro might ask is, "What's your Budget?"

When you ask the customer to tell you what payment they have in mind, they're never ever going to tell you the highest figure they can pay, or the highest number they've discussed with each other. If they've agreed with each other that they can afford $750 a month payments, they'll tell the Sales Pro their budget is $500 a month. Customers never tell you the highest number they can pay.

That's why most Sales Pros, and even Sales Managers, start the deal too low, because we found out too much. We overqualified the customers, and then we end up trying to 'Bump' them.

FEAR OF THE MONEY

The number one #1 reason that deals get blown is 'Fear of the Money'. This is an original Ziegler concept, but I assure you it's true. Most Sales Pros, no matter how experienced, have this fear

Remember, A Payment Is The F&I Department's Invoice

If a sales manager insists on quoting the payment, then you have also accepted full responsibility for the F&I production and profitability in your dealership. A sales manager or desk manager who continually quotes stripped-out payments (at the buy rate) to the customers must accept responsibility for sabotaging the profitability of the F&I department. The F&I department and the F&I managers represent a substantial and important profit center for the dealership and the dealer as well as a vehicle to control the customer and to get the car delivered.

An F&I manager is not a clerk, and they are not the sales manager's secretary. F&I is a viable profit center. When a sales manager or a desk manager or a Sales Professional strips all of the finance profit out of a deal, that sales manager, desk manager or Sales Professional has gotten weak with someone else's money.

It has often been said that... **"A Good F&I Manager Ought TO Be Able To Sell Up."**

Unfortunately, that is usually said by a weak sales manager who is guilty of blatantly stripping away F&I profits because he/she has weak skills and needs someone to blame it on. No one likes to have their invoice given away before they have a chance to sell their products. How would you, as a sales manager, like to have someone giving all of your customers a copy of the invoice and the appraisal on their trade before you started to negotiate?

How would it feel if someone kept disclosing your invoice or ACV and saying...

"A Good Sales Manager Ought to be Able to Sell Up?"

68

Sales Professionals Coaching the Customer or Working Against the Manager

A good Sales Manager needs to be aware of a Sales Professional's negative behavior during negotiation. We hate to admit it, but there is always a possibility that the Sales Pro has already committed to the customer and given the customer numbers, but they have not told the manager.

There are always Sales Pros who are afraid of the numbers, and don't want to present the Manager's proposal to the customer, especially if they've been overly talking about the numbers with the customer. Fear of the Money blows deals!

a) Managing their own deals
b) Premature commitment to customer
c) Sneaking the customer out without a turnover to a manager
d) Talking the manager out of raising the customer
e) Talking the manager out of selling the car
f) Manipulating the sale, coaching the customer to work against the manager
g) Coming back to the desk too quickly after the manager sent in the counter- proposal, not enough time selling the prospect on the proposal
h) Doesn't want to take the counterproposal back in to the prospect
i) Afraid to ask for the money
j) Intimidated by the customer
k) Afraid to ask for the order. Coming back with no signature, no money
l) There's something the Sales Professional hasn't told the manager
m) Arguing with the manager about the way they want to do it.
n) Not telling the prospect what they rehearsed with the manager at the desk. Doing their own thing once they go back into the prospect.

o) Not sitting down when they go back in with the prospect
p) Nervous, lack of confidence in what they are trying to do
q) Weak facial expressions and body language, stammering

DESKING THE DEAL

There are habits the best managers develop that have become second nature. If we believe that Down-Payment is the key to profitability as well as getting the deal approved by the finance institution with the best possible terms in the customer's best benefit, then cash down payment is in the customer's best interest as well as the dealership's. A good desk manager will always get the money from the customer while you're working the deal. Certainly before you send in a counterproposal.

Customer says: Okay, I'll be putting down $1500.00, down payment.

Sales Professional immediately says: "Great, write that check to Great Dealer Motors"

Customer says: "I'm not prepared to do that right now."

Sales Pro Says: "No problem, Mr./Mrs. Customer, actually our management would like to see a good faith retainer if your sending them a counteroffer. If for any reason we don't do business, we'll give it back right away. We have no intention of keeping your down payment if there is no deal."

Sales Manager: Send the Sales Professional back for the money if they return to the sales desk without a good faith retainer. Old timers used to call this 'Ernest Money'.

There are things we can negotiate other than money

  a) Cost of trade-in repairs
  b) Adding and removing equipment
  c) Throw in something extra instead of discount …
      promotional items, free television, game tickets, restaurant gift certificates, etc.

DESKING THE DEAL (CONT)

There are habits the best managers develop that have become second nature. If we believe that Down-Payment is the key to profitability as well as getting the deal approved by the finance institution with the best possible terms in the customer's best benefit, then cash down payment is in the customer's best interest as well as the dealership's. A good desk manager will always get the money from the customer while you're working the deal. Certainly before you send in a counterproposal

Do not tell the Sales Pro what the appraisal figure is while the deal is working, even if you are an A-to-Z Dealership. The manager controls the numbers.

As a manager, I want the Sales Professional to bring to the desk everything the customer brought with them to make the deal.

  a) Trade-in keys
  b) Driver's licenses
  c) Title to trade-in
  d) Tag slip to trade-in
  e) Insurance card from their wallet
  f) Down Payment Money, we don't want deposits, we want the full amount of the down payment they say they're putting down.
  g) Paperwork on trade-in, original contract, payment book, etc.
  h) Insurance policy, invoice, items from glove compartment that pertain to the sale, extended warranty policy, etc.

DESKING THE DEAL (CONT)

The Scripted Four-square

For 48 years, anyone who knows me will say that I am the absolute master of four-square. Many people even said I invented it, which is not true. No matter what you choose to believe, ask anyone that's taken my seminars, I am the best there is, the best there ever was, and the best there ever will be when it comes to working a car deal, legally, ethically, customer-friendly, and high profit.

Many people have tried to take credit for inventing the four-square, and they'd be mistaken. I don't want to call them a liar in writing, but if you ask me privately, I might say something different. The four-square was actually invented by a Texan named Ernie 'Tex' Pritchett. I believe his training company was called Control Incorporated. He and I were casual friends, I spoke to him and his adult son often back in the late 80s, early 90s. I didn't invent it, I just perfected it.

As an alternative to the four-square, many dealerships began using the 'Payment Matrix' worksheets that are in most CRMs. The Payment Matrix is a worksheet with 9 or more Payments matched up with mathematically correct corresponding Down Payments. It seems only logical that a Sales Pro would show the customers the matrix of payments and down payments and they'd choose the one that best suited them.

That's Great! Except, it doesn't work.

You heard me, it just doesn't work, and it never did. Think about it. I've had managers argue with me in class defending the Payment Matrix because that's what they were using, but eventually, they all had to admit it doesn't work. Sounds good, in theory, you'd think the customers would choose a payment and a corresponding down payment that mathematically fit the payment they chose.

Like I said, it sounds good, but in reality, people usually chose the zero down payment option with a low payment that didn't mathematically equate to the zero down payment they chose. Every time the manager had to drag out the green Sharpie and explain that it doesn't work that way.

The four-square was still superior in profitability, but it was getting a bad reputation because so many managers and Sales Pros were misusing the tool.

It was usually just four boxes hand drawn on a worksheet with Payment, Trade-in, Down Payment, and Payment in the four squares. It's terribly amateurish to use something that crude to do business on a $40,000 - $100,000 item like a new car. Like I said, it had a bad reputation and it looked 'stoopid'. It certainly didn't do much to help our image.

Years ago, as a manager, it occurred to me that different Sales Pros presented the figures differently with the customers. No matter how meticulously I coached them at the sales desk, many of them struggled with the word tracks in the presentation of the figures, especially the new hires and the 'Green Peas'.

They looked stiff and the words came out stilted and unnaturally. They had tried to memorize it, but the word tracks are complex, and they'd forget parts that were important. I've always said, it needs to sound like 'Conversation' not 'Memorization'.

AND, of course, the 'Old Pros' that felt they knew more than the managers, would leave the sales desk, and go to the customers saying whatever they wanted to say. They certainly weren't saying the scripted word tracks the manager coached them on.

Sometimes the 'Old Car Dogs' were actually coaching the customers, or maybe they had already discussed figures with the customers, and they really didn't intend to present the figures from the desk. Maybe the 'Fear of the Money' syndrome had kicked in.

Regardless, almost nobody was presenting the four-square presentations the way the desk manager had structured it. That's when it struck me like a bolt of lightning. Why don't we just print the entire word tracks on the worksheet?

It was quite simple actually. I printed out the word tracks with fill-in-the-blanks for the numbers. The desk manager would just fill in the numbers or print it from the CRM onto the worksheet. Many dealerships installed the worksheet into their CRMs.

All of a sudden, the numbers soared, front and back profits were higher than ever before. Even a brand-new salesperson could present the numbers with confidence because they were reading it to the customer.

DESKING THE DEAL (CONT)

AND an added bonus to doing it this way was that the customers trusted the worksheets that were preprinted this way. They felt comfortable that everyone was getting the same presentation of the figures without prejudice or the whims of the Sales Manager. It was certainly more trustworthy than smiley faces and "You Win" written with a green Sharpie. My consulting clients were successfully using this scripted four-square in BMW, Mercedes, and Lexus Dealerships, because better educated consumers felt comfortable with it. Customers also had a trust factor with the scripted four-square because they were reading it along with the Sales Pro, so they knew we weren't trying to slide something in on them or misrepresenting anything. I had left a space under the payment amount to write in the interest rate, or the residual so we could convert the deal and present a lease.

One reason this worksheet is so successful and high profit is because it doesn't look like a four-square. Most dealerships were still writing the numbers into the blanks by hand, and then scratching them out, and finishing the deal with a green Sharpie during the negotiation. Other dealerships were printing the scripted four-square out of the CRM with the numbers printed in.

Many dealerships have designed different types of worksheets around the scripted part with different types of information. I own scripted four-square, but I welcome anyone to use it to work car deals with customers, regardless of what copywrite is on my books and forms. The only people who may Not use it are businesses, other trainers and consultants, people writing books or articles, or anyone making a profit on it. It is by far the best and most profitable way to work a car deal. Here's an example of the Scripted Work Sheet.

This example of the Scripted four-square is for new car deals. Of course, for used car deals it wouldn't include the 'cashback rebate', nor the 'preferred equipment package' discounts. You could choose to scratch that through, or program it as two separate forms in your CRM.

A. The market value of the vehicle you are purchasing is: $_____
This price includes a manufacturer preferred equipment package discount of: $_____
The Manufacturer is also giving you a cashback rebate of: $_____
Leaving you an adjusted sale price of: $_____ after all rebates and discounts.

B. Our professional buyers have looked at your car and, based on similar cars we have bought and sold recently, we are willing to buy your car today for: $_____ up to: $_____

C. We will be paying off your old vehicle as part of this Agreement up to $_____

D. Most lending institutions would like to see as much as 20% cash down payment for premium and preferred financial programs. In your case we would like to see $_____

E. This will make your estimated monthly investment _____ payments between $_____ and $_____ a month.

Buyer(s) and Seller agree that any additional payment the lien holder requires to obtain title is responsibility of the Buyer(s)

Notice, there is a space directly under the payment range to write in, or preprogram to print in the CRM, the interest rate, or the residual amount if it is a lease. Many dealerships require the customers initials next to the disclaimer at the bottom to disclose that the customer understands that, if the payoff on the trade-in is higher than the estimate, that they will be responsible for the difference.

The purpose of the Scripted version is full disclosure and a customer-friendly disclosure and understanding of the figures during the negotiation. As I mentioned previously, affluent and educated customers are more comfortable with this format than some kind of scribbled four-square on the back of the worksheet with a green Sharpie pen.

Many dealerships have been using the 'Payment/Down Payment Matrix' that shows the customer a choice of payments and down payments. Experienced managers will tell you that sounds good, but it doesn't work in the real world. Customers never choice the payment that corresponds with the correct down payment. This format is highly superior for high profitability with zero liability.

DESKING THE DEAL (CONT)

Basic Sale Presentation

The 'Market Value of the car you're buying is **XXXX**

Since this is one of our special program cars, our dealership or the manufacturer has discounted it **XXXX** dollars

(That's any Dealer Discounts, CPO discounts or 'Value Option Packages that are already included in the 'Market Value'.)

Leaving us with an adjusted market value of **XXXX**.

Our Professional Buyers (we never say used car manager, have a little class)

"Our Professional Buys have looked at the car that you're selling us and, based on cars just like it that we've brought and sold in the last ninety days, we're willing to buy it today for somewhere between **XXXX** and **XXXX**." (The key word in the word track is *"Looked at Your Car"*)

As you know, the banks in this area, including our manufacturer's lender, prefer a minimum of 20 percent cash down payment. So we're going to need a cash down payment from you now; at least **XXXX**.

(The words, "As You Know", are very important)

Which will make your monthly investment fall between **XXX** and **XXX** , that's a $10.00 range, depending on which lender and your personal credit history.

Write me that check for **XXXX** Make it out to the dealership and we'll get with the Financial Manager and get your paperwork started.

Customer Says What's You Interest Rate?

This is a question every reasonable customer is most likely to ask.

Customer says, *"What's the Interest Rate?"* We really never want to avoid a reasonable question BUT we never want to ever lie or mislead the customer. A salesperson on the lot is Not capable of answering this question without more information. BUT, If a customer starts hammering you, demanding to know the interest rate before they proceed or before they'll give you any information, most likely that customer is probably severely "Credit Challenged".

In other words, they probably have bad credit and want you to commit before they tell you anything about themselves.

Here's the answer. Customer says, "What's your best interest rate?"

Sales Pro says, "Mr. Customer, as you know different people qualify for different financial programs, it depends on two things."

"It Depends on Your Credit History and the Amount of Your Down Payment"

1. As you know, the amount of your down payment that most lending institutions would like to see is a minimum of 20% CASH DOWN for PERFERRED FINANCIAL TERMS. Never tell the customer that the financial source 'Requires 20% down'. Always say, "They's like to see 20% down for preferred financial programs.

    It also depends on your personal credit history - Under the guidelines of Federal Regulation Z of the Fair Credit Disclosure Act, as a car Sales Professional, I am not allowed to know your personal credit history. I'm sure it's excellent. (although you may suspect it's Not) We have several people here, our Financial Managers, who are licensed and bonded, educated in finance, who are able to discuss your personal credit history with you in privacy and present programs, which you qualify for.

2. Right now, my sales manager uses interest rates and payment averages based on average credit and interest rates in our area as determined by national authority, **http://www. Bankrate.com** , that's fair, isn't it?

3. Customer says: "Is Zero Percent Available?" (This is a trap, be careful)

    Sales Pro says: "Yes Sir/Ma'am, it's one of many Financial Programs for Extremely Qualified Buyers. At the proper times our Financial Managers will show you all of the programs for which you personally qualify.

Customer Says Give Me Your Best Price

Sales Pro Says, "My Best Price? No Problem! "I'm so glad you asked ! Here at Good Dealer, price is our specialty."

"There's a big sale going on right now; I am sure that's why you are here today. Did you come in because our advertised specials, or perhaps you've spoken to one of our representatives?"

"I'm sure Price is important to you, and we're never going to lose your business if Price is the issue."

"Our dealership policy is not only to get you our very best Price, BUT we've going to give you all of the information you need to make an informed and intelligent decision. Not only the best Price, but the interest rate, the monthly payment, the amount we'll pay for your trade-in, and the alternative lease payment. Everything you need to make an intelligent decision … with No Pressure to Buy. That's fair, isn't it?"

(The phrase, "No Pressure to Buy." Must be in the track. The "Fairness Challenge at the end of that track is one of the strongest closes there is. Nobody wants to be unfair.

The Sales Pro then says, "All we require is that we select (and drive) a specific vehicle before we discuss the figures, fair enough? It's part of our customer satisfaction program. The manufacturer will be asking if you drove the vehicle as part of your dealer satisfaction survey."

The strongest one line close that Jim Ziegler ever invented is, "The Now Commitment close."

Sales Pro says, "Mister Customer, if you could own this car on your own terms, you'd own it Now, wouldn't you?"

Sales Pro says, "Great let's select a vehicle and drive it, then we'll get with the management and discuss your terms, fair enough?"

Basic Sale Presentation
Value Option Package

The 'Market Value of the car you're buying is **XXXX**

Since this is one of our special program cars, our dealership or the manufacturer has discounted it **XXXX** dollars

This is a car with a Value-Option package on the window sticker where the manufacturer has discounted options or thrown them in a package discount. That's any Dealer Discounts, CPO discounts or 'Value Option Packages that are already included in the 'Market Value'. We're just telling the consumer it's been pre-discounted by the manufacturer already.

That leaves us with an adjusted market value of **XXXX**.

Our Professional Buyers have looked at your trade-in, the car you're selling us.

(we never say used car manager put a number on it or appraised it, have a little class)

"Our Professional Buys have looked at the car that you're selling us as part of this deal and, based on cars just like it that we've brought and sold in the last ninety days, we're willing to buy it today for somewhere between **XXXX** and **XXXX**."

(The key word in the word track is *"Looked at Your Car"*)

As you know, the banks in this area, including our manufacturer's lender, prefer a minimum of 20 percent cash down payment. So we're going to need a cash down payment from you now; at least **XXXX**.

(The words, "As You Know", are very important)

Which will make your monthly investment fall between **XXX** and **XXX** , that's a $10.00 range, depending on which lender and your personal credit history.

Write me that check for **XXXX** Make it out to the dealership and we'll get with the Financial Manager and get your paperwork started.

Basic Sale Presentation

The 'Market Value of the car you're buying is **XXXX**

Since this is one of our special program cars, our dealership or the manufacturer has discounted it **XXXX** dollars

(That's any Dealer Discounts, CPO discounts or 'Value Option Packages that are already included in the 'Market Value'.)

Leaving us with an adjusted market value of **XXXX**.

In the Trade-in line we have written the words, "Payoff Included".

Sales Pro says: "Any deal we agree on today will include paying off your old car, to Happy Employees Credit Union up to **XXXX**." (estimated payoff figure)

(The key words in this word track are, "Any deal we make today will include paying off your old car up to … ")

As you know, the banks in this area, including our manufacturer's lender, prefer a minimum cash down payment. In your case, my manager estimates they'll be looking for a cash down payment from you now of at least **XXXX**. (notice we did Not say 20%, since it's higher than that)

(The words, "As You Know", are very important)

Which will make your monthly investment fall between **XXX** and **XXX** , that's a $10.00 range, depending on which lender and your personal credit history.

Write me that check for **XXXX** Make it out to the dealership and we'll get with the Financial Manager and get your paperwork started.

THE UPSIDE-DOWN TRADE-IN NEGATIVE EQUITY WORD TRACK

Manager should have given the Sales Professional a **"Hit Figure"** to work toward. (approximate acceptable payment counteroffer) This is so the Sales Pro knows what payment and down payment to work toward.

In other words, I might say to the Sales Pro: "I'll need a down payment on this deal of at least $4500, and a payment agreement of at least $625 a month."

Customer says, "How much are you giving me for my trade-in? What does 'payoff included' mean? It's worth a least **XXXX** CPV."

(Customer's Perceived Valve for Trade-In)

Sales Pro says, "Gosh Mr. Customer, that sounds rather high to me. Would you mind sharing how you arrived at that figure?"

(It's important to know how the customer arrived at their CPV)

Sales Pro says, "Actually Mr./Mrs. Customer, my manager said you're payoff is rather high.

(don't tell them they're upside down or try to explain negative equity, just say their payoff is rather high.)

Sales Pro continues, "And because your payoff is high, we don't have an exact figure on it so far. Our managers are on the phones right now calling other professional buyers around the state that specialize in paying the highest prices for cars like yours.

So while they're shopping your trade-in to get you the best value, let's work on the payment and the down payment, I'll tell you what Mr. Customer. Since the payment is going to be the ultimate factor on which you're going to base your decision, let's work on the

payment. and if we can arrive at a payment and down payment that our managers are comfortable with, Then, we'll pay whatever we have to for your old car to make the deal. Fair enough?"

Customer says, "I don't know."

THE UPSIDE-DOWN TRADE-IN NEGATIVE EQUITY WORD TRACK (CONT)

Sales Pro continues, "Let me ask you this, I don't know if we could go as high as <u>CPV</u> but if my manager paid a lot more to buy your car; is the figure we discussed, **XXX** okay for your monthly payments?"

Customer says, "No way. I can't pay a payment that high"

Sales Pro says, "In other words, you're not going to pay a payment as high as **XXX**, no matter how much we pay for your car?"

Customer says, "That's right, that payment is way too high for us."

Sales Pro says, "Sir/Ma'am, that is an accelerated high-equity payment, 48 months. Many people prefer that so you can pay off the car sooner, you can trade more frequently, and it saves a quit a lot in interest. I'm authorized to offer you 60-month financing which will lower your payments at least $20 a month, so if I can get your payments to **XXX**, will that do it?

Customer says, I need payments of **XXX** at most.

NOW, the customer has given you a payment offer, that is higher than they would have said if You hadn't thrown out that higher number first. This is the time work the highest payment they'll offer. Remember, no pressure, conversation, and persuasion.

Sales Pro says, "Okay Mr./Mrs. Customer, if my management will agree to that payment, regardless of how much we have to pay for your trade to make that work out, do we have a deal?"

Customer says, "Yes, I'll do that payment." (whatever they agreed to)

Sales Pro says, "Great write me that check for **XXXX** and I'll take that to the management to get everything started."

Customer says, "Wait a second, I don't have that much money to put down."

Sales Pro, surprised look says, "Oh I assumed you were planning to put 20% down payment **XXXX**. As I mentioned before the banks are going to be looking for a cash down payment since your payoff is high. We're estimating they'll be looking for **XXXX** but I'm sure we might persuade them to take less, how close to that can you come up with? How much do you feel you're going to be short?

Customer says, "I can come up with **XXXX**.

Sales Pro says, "Can you come up with as much as **XXXX** if you had to? You know if you absolutely had to?

Customer says, "Well, I suppose if I had to."

Sales Pro says, "I think you're going to have to. So, write me that check for **XXXX**... (That's called the 'If You Had To' bump, a Ziegler original.)

Now remember, we're not hiding anything here. The reason we're doing it this way is because when a customer is upside down in their trade-in payoff, it really doesn't matter what the figures are if the lending institution doesn't accept the equity situation, which means down payment to cover the negative equity and put this deal into positive equity. In other words they're probably upside down because they didn't put down payment into the last car they financed.

"Our figures are based on the highest and the lowest amounts we've bought or sold cars like yours for in the last ninety days. If I could get you the higher number, do we have a deal?"

Customer... *"That's right."*

"I'll tell you what Mr. Customer. Since the payment is going to be the ultimate factor on which you're going to base your decision, let's work on the payment. When we arrive at a payment that you and my manager can agree upon, if we agree that we have a deal. Then, we'll pay whatever we have to for your old car to make the deal. Fair enough?"

Payment Objection

Customer says, "That payment is too high."

Sales Pro says, "Mr. Customer, you do realize that's an accelerated, high equity payment, don't you?"

Remember , the Sales Manager has started the deal at 48 months or maybe 60 months on the first set of figures. Never at 72 months or 84 months on the first pass. This is accelerated equity, much in the customers' best benefit, as well as ours.

Customer says, *"A what?"*

Sales Pro says, "It's an accelerated, high equity payment. Short term financing. My manager has set it up so that you can pay the car off in four years or less. You'll save thousands in interest, can trade more frequently for a newer car, and not be suffering with negative equity.

We did this for your benefit. Most people prefer this, even though the payments are slightly higher. It's a national trend. Many people are even financing their home for shorter terms, say fifteen years instead of thirty. All of our retail payments are quoted on short-term repayment as well as our other alternative financial programs.

(The manager may have included a lease payment on the worksheet)

Sales Pro says, "Did you want a payment lower than that?"
(As if you couldn't believe they wouldn't want the higher payment with accelerated equity. Raise eyebrow in a facial expression of disbelief)

Customer says, "I sure do want a lower payment?"

Sales Pro says, "No Problem! We have many ways to lower your payments. I'm sure your credit is excellent, and, with your good

credit, we can get longer terms and lower payments, or I can check with my management for one of our special alternative programs, perhaps a lease? "

Sales Pro says, "What fair and reasonable payment did you have in mind?"

Sales Professional Evaluation Form

Sales Professional Name	Last Name	First Name
Evaluation Period (Month/Year)	Month	Year
Name		

Sales Performance Figures				
Last Month			Forecast	
	Actual	Objective		Objective
Number Of Ups			Number Of Ups	
Number Of Demos			Number Of Demos	
Units Sold			Units Sold	
Average Per Unit			Average Per Unit	
Total Comm.			Total Comm.	
Salary Bonus			Salary Bonus	
Total Earnings			Total Earnings	

FOCUS FOR THE MONTH:

Strengths

Weaknesses

Action Plan For Improvement

ACTION PLAN TO IMPROVE

SITUATION:

_____

MEASURE OF IMPROVEMENT?

_____

MEET TO REVIEW PROGRESS:

_____

WHO'S RESPONSIBLE:

_____

SIGNATURES: _____

Customer Trade-In Evaluation Survey

Date_____   1. ( ) 2. ( ) 3. ( ) 4. ( ) 5. ( ) 6. ( ) 7. ( ) 8. ( ) 9. ( ) 10. ( )

Year_____ Model_____.Manufacturer_____

Body Style_____Color_____

Vehicle Identification Number   _____

Customer Name_____ Sales Professional _____

1. Mileage on Odometer_____ mileage accurate?   ☐ Yes   ☐ No
2. Do You Have the Title?   ☐ Yes   ☐ No
3. Is this a Salvaged Title?   ☐ Yes   ☐ No
4. Is the Title Free and Clear?   ☐ Yes   ☐ No
5. Lien Holder_____Estimated Payoff._____
6. Has This Car Had Any Major Mechanical Repairs?   ☐ Yes   ☐ No
   What Type of Repairs?_____

7. Has This Car Ever Had Any Collision Damage?   ☐ Yes   ☐ No
   What Type of Collision Damage and What Was the Cost of the Repairs?

   _____
   _____

8. Was the Vehicle Purchased New?   ☐ Yes   ☐ No
9. Has this Car Been Smoked In?   ☐ Yes   ☐ No
10. Has this Car Been Used in Towing?   ☐ Yes   ☐ No
11. Date of Last Tune-Up?_____
12. Date of Last Oil Change?_____
13. Has the Oil Been Changed Every 4000 Miles?   ☐ Yes   ☐ No
14. Records of Required Maintenance History?   ☐ Yes   ☐ No
15. How Many Miles on the Current Tires?_____
16. Is This Car Equipped With a Spare and a Jack?   ☐ Yes   ☐ No
17. Does This Car Have a Warranty In Force Currently?   ☐ Yes   ☐ No
18. Manufacturer's Warranty? ☐ Yes   ☐ No Remaining Miles_____
19. Extended Service Contract? ☐ Yes   ☐ No   Remaining Miles_____
20. Environmental Protection Package... Rust Proofing?   ☐ Yes   ☐ No

Paint Protection?   ☐ Yes   ☐ No   Interior or Fabric Protection? D Yes   ☐ No

I certify that I believe all of the information I have provided to be true and accurate.
I give permission to appraise and evaluate my car.

X _____ Date_____

SAMPLE EMPLOYMENT AD
(from the 1990's)

$65,000 AVERAGE EXPECTATION
WANTED IMMEDIATELY!

5 MEN OR WOMEN FOR EXECUTIVE SALES POSITION

- Company Car
- Paid Insurance w/Life and Dental
- 401k Plan
- Quality Work Schedule
- Five Day Work Week
- One Weekend Off Every Month
- Advancement Opportunity
- Career Path into Management
- *$1,000 Per Week Minimum Guarantee During Initial Six-Week Training Period
- **$3,000 Sign Up Bonus for Experienced Auto Sales Professionals
- Our Top Performers Earn an Average of $12,000 Per Month

---

*Must Have Documented Successful Sales Track Record In Any Profession Required to Qualify for $1,000.00 Guarantee.

**$3,000.00 Sign up Bonus for Professional Automobile Sales Professionals with a Strong Documented Track Record.

Any Dealership Name
Call Cindy or Ron (123) 555-1234
E-mail: cindy@anydealership.com

Run With The Big Dogs Pay Plan Example of Multi-Level Pay Plan (from1997)

Are you ready to run with the big dogs?
The following is a career-oriented pay plan that some of the country's leading dealers are now adopting. It's structured in tiers so as a salesperson's performance increases, he or she is rewarded with higher commissions as well as paid travel, flextime, a laptop, dinner with the dealer and other perks.

Jim Ziegler, Ziegler Supersystems   800.726.0510   www.zieglersupersystems.com

Entry Level:
- 25% front-end commission or $500, whichever is more.
- Minimum 6 sales per month.
- Sales training 1 hour per day, perform lot duties and only take in-store ups (no incoming phone leads).
- Must advance to Professional Level within 90 days.
- Receives $75 minimum commission.

Professional Level:
- 28% front-end commission.
- Must have graduated from entry level or minimum 1-year sales experience at another store.
- Minimum 12 vehicles sales per month at store gross, front- and back-end average for at least two consecutive months each quarter (Penalty: Salesperson goes back to entry-level if gross/production threshold isn't met).
- Sales training 1 hour twice a week, perform lot duties and may take phone-ups.
- Receives $200 each month toward personal car.
- Receives $75 minimum commission.

Executive Level:
- 30% commission.
- Minimum 17 sales per month at or above store's gross, front- and back-end average for two consecutive months each quarter (Penalty: Salesperson goes back to professional level if gross/production threshold isn't met.).
- One-week paid vacation at $750 plus coach airfare for two to anywhere in the U.S. after maintaining executive level status for one year.
- One weekend off each month from noon Friday until noon Monday—with no weekdays off during that week.
- Laptop computer with professional contact management system after one year at executive level.
- Demo vehicle (with personal insurance) and cell phone (plus $50 towards bill) for 6 consecutive months at executive level. Note: The cell phone number must appear on business cards.
- Invitation with guest or spouse to monthly dinner with dealer at upscale restaurant.
- $100 flat fee (no split) when assisting sold and delivered deals, and full compensation for "house" deals, which aren't counted toward monthly quotas.
- Engraved Rolex watch for maintaining executive level status for three consecutive years.

Master Level:
- 35% commission.
- Minimum 30 sales front- and back-end average (Penalty: If the salesperson fails to meet either the unit production or gross thresholds for two of any four consecutive months, the salesperson moves back to the appropriate sales level).
- No set schedule, provided salesperson maintains the unit/gross profit requirements and submits a written schedule to sales managers a week in advance.
- 2 weeks paid vacation at $1000/week and coach airfare for two to anywhere in the U.S. or Mexico.
- $100 minimum commission.
- Laptop computer, if they don't have one that includes contact management software for maintaining master status for six consecutive months.
- Invitation with guest or spouse to monthly dinner with dealer.
- Full-time administrative assistant and private office after maintaining master status for six months.
- Demo vehicle with dealer-provided insurance after maintaining master status for six months.
- Cell phone with $100 toward bill for maintaining master status for six months. Note: The cell phone number must appear on their business cards.
- $100 flat fee (no split) when assisting sold and delivered deals, and full compensation for "house" deals, which aren't counted toward monthly quotas.
- Engraved Rolex watch for maintaining master status for two consecutive years.
- Personal Web site, tied to the store's site, for maintaining master status for six months.

Customer Proposal

Date: _____

(1) Buyer(s) / Purchaser(s) Name(s) as it will appear on the title

_____

(2) Vehicle Selected _____ Stock Number _____

(3) Sales Representative_____

(4) Description of Vehicle New - Pre-owned - Certified Pre-owned - Model Year _____

(5) Manufacturer_____ Model _____

(6) Style _____ Color _____

(7) Odometer Mileage _____

(8) VIN Number _____ (17 digits)

(9) Description of Trade Model Year _____Manufacturer_____

(10) Model _____ Odometer Mileage _____

(11) VIN Number _____ (17 digits)

A. The market value of the vehicle you are purchasing is: $_____
This price includes a manufacturer preferred equipment package discount of: $_____
The Manufacturer is also giving you a cashback rebate of: $_____
Leaving you an adjusted sale price of: $_____
after all rebates and discounts.

B. Our professional buyers have looked at your car and, based on similar cars we have bought and sold recently, we are willing to buy your car today for: $_____ up to: $_____

C. We will be paying off your old vehicle as part of this Agreement up to $_____

D. Most lending institutions would like to see as much as 20% cash down payment for premium and preferred financial programs. In your case we would like to see $_____

E. This will make your estimated monthly investment _____ payments between $_____ and $_____ a month.

Buyer(s) and Seller agree that any additional payment the lien holder requires to obtain title is responsibility of the Buyer(s)

Sales Representatives Cannot Accept This Offer Nor Does A Sales Representative Have The Authority To Obligate Seller In Any Manner. Any Offer From The Customer(S) To The Seller Is Not Binding Unless Accepted In Writing By An Officer Of The Seller Or Sales Manager. I certify all information on this application is accurate and complete to the best of my knowledge. I authorize the seller and any financial institution that does business with the seller to review my application and creditworthiness and to conduct an investigation of my credit history and my employment history.

(12) **Initials**_____ _____

In that different consumers qualify for different financial programs depending on credit history and the amount of down payment, your exact financial programs and payment options will be discussed with you in privacy by one of our qualified financial managers.

X _____ Applicant Signature Required

X _____ Joint Applicant Signature Required

Buyer(s) and Seller agree that any additional payment the lien holder requires to obtain title is responsibility of the Buyer(s).

Truth in Lending Act (TILA)

Disclosure of Federal Regulation Z
Title 15, Chapter 41, Subchapter 1 : Part B
Part B – Credit Transactions

This consumer acknowledgement of disclosure is in additional clarification to the retail installment contract, hereinafter referred to as "the contract", pertaining to the sale and financials of a motor vehicle more particularly described as follows:

Seller_____   Buyer(s)_____

Dateofcontract:_____   **Co-Buyer**_____

Vehicle Description

Year	Make	Model	Vehicle Identification Number
_____	_____	_____	_____

Number of payments	When payments are due	Annual Percentage Rate
_____	_____	_____%

Optional Protection Items

Accept Initials   **Decline Initials**

Accept		Decline
_____	Parts and Labor Agreement (VSC)	_____
_____	Key Fob Replacement	_____
_____	Automotive Theft Deterrent (Etch)	_____
_____	Guaranteed Asset Protection (GAP)	_____
_____	Environmental Protection Package	_____
_____	Tire and Road Hazard Protection	_____
_____	Pre-Paid Scheduled Service(Maintenance)	

FDIC Law, Regulations, Related Acts
6500-FDIC Consumer Protection p. 6641 part 226-Truth in Lending
Subpart C- Closed end Credit section 226.17; 226.18; 226.20; 226.22

Consumer protection laws require that the above-listed protection options were fully explained. Any acceptance of these items is not a condition of loan approval nor required to qualify for a certain interest rate or term. Furthermore, any declination of these protection options serves as a waiver of liability ; by signatures affixed buyer(s) acknowledge these products and services have been fully explained and agree to release and hold harmless this dealership from any liability or damages arising from claimed that would have been covered by these items. Any applicable manufacturer warranties remain in effect. Additional regulation Z disclosure appears on the retain installment contract

Buyer signature
_____

Co Buyer Signature
_____

Dealership Representative
_____

www.ingramcontent.com/pod-product-compliance
Lightning Source LLC
Chambersburg PA
CBHW021604210326
41599CB00010B/595